M000033887

# FEAST AFTER

# THE SPIRIT

*POETRY*

Talmage
Gorringe

9/26/2011

## L. TALMAGE GORRINGE

COPYRIGHT © 2004 BY TALMAGE GORRINGE.

LIBRARY OF CONGRESS NUMBER: 2004091749

ISBN:   SOFTCOVER   1-4134-5174-8

All rights reserved. No part of this book may be reproduced or transmitted in any form or by any means, electronic or mechanical, including photocopying, recording, or by any information storage and retrieval system, without permission in writing from the copyright owner.

This book was printed in the United States of America.

To order additional copies of this book, contact:
Xlibris Corporation
1-888-795-4274
www.Xlibris.com
Orders@Xlibris.com
23087

# PREFACE

## (L. TALMAGE GORRINGE)

Tal was born Nov. 11, 1976. Do you know why this day was special? It was Veteran's Day of the Bicentennial year of our country's independence. Besides being born on a special day, Tal was a special kid. He was a gutsy 5-year old who liked to ride his big wheel down the sidewalk by taking off the seat, kneeling on the big wheel and pushing with his foot. That way he could go faster. We called him "a bull in a china cupboard."

We were sledding at Sugar House Park, Dec. 31, 1981. Tal wanted to take the Glad-a-Boggan down the hill himself. Mom begged him to let her go with him. Grandma pleaded with him to let her go with him. Tal said, "no." He had to go by himself. Mom watched him start down the hill. His plastic runnerless sled headed for the railing post, the one kids used to pull themselves up the hill. Kawham!! He was going about 50-70 mph when his head hit the post. Mom gave the baby to grandma and ran down the hill. Tal was bleeding from his nose, mouth and someplace else, maybe the back of his head. Someone called an ambulance. A lady led a prayer circle and shortly after an Elder of the Church of Jesus Christ of Latter-day Saints blessed Tal that he would remain alive until the doctors could help him.

The doctor's didn't give much hope at the hospital. They removed the left side of his skull to allow for swelling of the brain. After 10 days the doctors took him out of a drug-induced coma. He was paralyzed on the right side and had lost his speech. His head was swollen or sunken depending on how the shunt was working. The doctors and nurses called him "the miracle child."

It is this gutsy little boy, (I call him little because he is 26 years old and is 4 feet and 8 inches tall) who defeated the odds and survived that accident, is who writes this book of poetry. This young man walks with a crutch and uses a wheelchair. He not only writes poetry, but he has been on a mission to Tempe, Arizona. He attended Salt Lake Community College Skill Center, with studies in Medical Records.

In this horrific accident, the left side of his brain was damaged. Today Tal has developed the right side of his brain, which is the creative side. Therefore he enjoys writing poetry, he has deep spiritual experiences and thoughts, I hope you appreciate the talents of this young man.

3

# TOUCH THE TOUCH

### L. TALMAGE GORRINGE

Touch the touch, where it brings
happiness to your eternal perfection.
Touch the touch, where ye cannot touch without
the help of our Father in Heaven
and his Son, Jesus Christ, to bring peace and joy to your loved ones and you.
Touch the touch that makes you feel
the love that lasts forever and ever,
in the kingdom of God,
to bring Pure happiness and great joy to your sphere.
Touch the touch, where ye claim all that
God possesses; to create worlds,
animals, trees, Shrubbery, man, and woman,
that ye may create a help meet to assist you in
beautifying and replenishing this land to your likeness.
Touch the touch, which are private
and sacred to one's self;
to feed the need of feeling
physical and romantic enjoyment.
Touch the touch, whereas ye
may have a relationship with a person of the opposite sex.
Touch the touch, where ye may respect the
parts that are sacred and true to the people
who strive to be like God (The Father)
and his Son, Jesus Christ
(The Savior),
to receive eternal Happiness and
a great love for all man kind, and to possess all that he has.

# FEEL THE FEEL

## L. TALMAGE GORRINGE

Feel the feel, which few have felt;
it invites the
holy spirit of God into your Life,
which bringeth the knowledge and wisdom
of the plan of happiness and salvation,
to have you return back to our Father's presence,
to dwell with Him in The Most High, in the Celestial kingdom.
Feel the feel, which our Father feels,
which bringeth unto you the feelings of a
loving parent who wants you to return back to Him,
and to give back unto Him all that he has given unto you,
so you can inherit the
kingdom of God and much more.
Feel the feel, which angers our Father
and his Son, Jesus Christ, to try to help you
understand why this life is so important unto them,
to bring you back into their sphere,
and to live in happiness for all eternity.


# LOVE KEEPS ME ALIVE

## L. TALMAGE GORRINGE

Love keeps me alive through acts of kindness to others.
Love keeps me alive through bringing peace to people who are hurting or are in pain;
it pains me to see a stranger in pain, therefore, comfort him and I will be happy forever.
People who love others, are gentle to their feelings, and desire to help others become happy again.
As you love, you will be loved, therefore, never stop loving.

# THIS IS THE LAND

L. TALMAGE GORRINGE

This is the land where God dwells,

pure and peaceful above all other lands;

to bless and answer prayers

to all those who hearken to His voice.

This is the land where we dwell with God,

where there are no wars, rumors of wars, or temptations.

This is the land wherein, you will create kingdoms, palaces, mansions, and worlds;

to bring gold, silver, and all manner of precious things into

this marvelous place.

This is the land whereby you will live with our Father in Heaven

and his Son, Jesus Christ

for eternity.

This is the land where God

dwells amongst His children.

This is the land where peace and

humility abide for eternity.

This is the land where no foul

language is spoken,

no guile spreading from one

person to the next.

This is the land where happiness,

joy, peace, and love abide for eternity.

# THE POWER OF LOVE

### L. Talmage Gorringe

The power of love may bring two
persons together or a whole nation,
depending upon how you look at life;
if you look at life with your heart and soul,
and through the eyes of God,
you won't bring just two persons together,
but you will bring a whole nation together;
to have love shared from one person to the
next until every person has felt
the sweet touch of your heart.

# ON TOP OF THE WORLD

### L. Talmage Gorringe

Few people have been on top of the world,
humility and peace will get you there.
Those who are on top of the
world are always in service to God and country.
Being on top of the world,
means obedience to the laws
and commandments of God,
to bring happiness, peace, and exaltation to the soul.
Being on top of the world you will find
God The Father and his Son, Jesus Christ,
to know that you have made it to
the Celestial kingdom, (The Highest of All Kingdoms).
He who is on top of the world is always aware of everything and everyone.
He who is on top of the world is spiritual and righteous and longs; to bring
love to all those who
will hearken to His words.

## WALKING IN THE MIDST OF . . .

### L. TALMAGE GORRINGE

Few people have walked in the midst of God's Kingdom;
to behold all that he has, and much more;
which he giveth unto you.
Because of your faith and obedience to the commandments,
laws and the promptings, ye have eternal life.
Walking in the midst of God's presence, makes you happy eternally,
because of the feelings He brings into your heart and soul,
to receive eternal life to your loved ones and you.
many people have walked in the midst of this world,
but only a few understand how to achieve the highest degree of glory, which is
through obedience to the commandments and laws of God, to know the Savior personally.


## I WILL DIE FOR YOU

### L. TALMAGE GORRINGE

The people who love the church and live
in accordance to the laws and
commandments of the Church of God,
find that they are willing to die for their beliefs,
and live forever in happiness with
God the Father and his Son, Jesus the Christ,
rather than to reject and live as a coward liveth.
For he who loves God,
will give his life for Him;
for without God we are naught,
therefore, give Heed to God,
and act upon His words;
if ye do this,
ye will receive a greater and higher love,
which is the love of God;
which is the home of the heart and soul,
(where ye ought to be).

# IF YOU GET THERE BEFORE I DO . . .

### L. TALMAGE GORRINGE

If you get there before I do, don't give up on me,
for the Lord needs me to accomplish a job which He commanded me,
to give peace to all, so they may have a chance to receive eternal life.
If you get there before I do, let your heart continue in love to God and country,
so you won't be tempted of the devil
to do something that will keep you
from entering the Celestial Kingdom.
If you get there before I do, don't wait up on me,
God is watching over me,
making sure nothing unfavorable is going to
happen to me on the greatest day of my life;
The day of judgement from my Father.


# NOBODY SEES IT BUT ME

### L. TALMAGE GORRINGE

Nobody sees what I see:
I see things the way they should be and not the way they are.
It gives me peace to know the will of the Father, who guides me to where he dwells.
The people who can see into the future are able to plan their lives in accordance to what the
world is going to be like, so they may be able to stay out of harms way
and live a life that is
Glorious to God (The Father).
We can all see the future, if we prepare most carefully,
and turn our hearts to God, so He can guide us back to His presence,
to bring unto us all that He has and much much more.
People who know what is going to happen in ten years or so,
have a hard time believing it,
so they live in shame and give their hearts to the world.

# ANGEL EYES

## L. TALMAGE GORRINGE

Angel eyes which I see are pure and of God,
they lieth not, but share truth all day long,
to bring repentance to all those who hearken and forsake their sins,
so they may be able to enter into God's kingdom when the time cometh.
The angel eyes bringeth peace to your eyes,
as you look into her eyes and see a person who is willing
to make you happy for all eternity, and to be with you for eternity.
The people who have angel eyes can see the truth in everyone,
and try to help them become truly happy with themselves,
so they may pass on the eyes of angels to all those who will look.
These angel eyes bring eternal life to all that would
look and feel the love which she
carries with her all the day long, every day.
Angel eyes are true and faithful to the Will of the Father,
and loves to talk to Him all the day long, every day.


# WEAPONS

## L. TALMAGE GORRINGE

Weapons are dangerous, and they can kill.
Sometimes people worship weapons as idols, they
try to get themselves to believe that this worshiping of idols will
actually help them out,
when, in fact, worshiping these idols can and will hurt you more than help you.
Weapons can be used for good things;
to kill animals for the food and fur,
so they may eat the meat and turn the fur into some warm useful clothes.
Weapons a lot of the time are misused;
to hold up a store, bank, or to force someone to go against their will.
Weapons can be used to remind people of the symbolic meaning which
God has assigned,
which will bring them closer to our Father in Heaven and his Son,
Jesus Christ, if they follow it.

## MIRACLES

L. TALMAGE GORRINGE

Miracles keep people alive
through the help of God
for without His help
we have no focus on how to live our lives.
Miracles bringeth peace and
happiness to our eternal realm,
so we may be close to our
Father in Heaven and his Son,
Jesus Christ, who will bring exaltation
to all who will hearken and live.
Miracles brighten our countenance,
and bring people unto you,
so they may learn of
the love that these miracles bring;
to try to live in accordance
to the way of eternal life with God.
Miracles bring us closer to our
Father in Heaven and his Son, Jesus Christ.

## SMILES

L. TALMAGE GORRINGE

A smile may put a person who is feeling sad
in a better mood so she may handle situations better.
People who have smiles on their faces
understand that they are making a difference in peoples' lives.
Each time you see a smile on a person
you wonder, what does she do to keep herself happy all the time.
A smile warms the soul;
it gives unto you peace, to let you
know that you to can feel this way.
A smile on a person's face makes you feel like
Anything is possible.

## PLAY BY THE BOOK

L. TALMAGE GORRINGE

Play by the book and you will be blessed eternally.
As you play by the book, you will become more like our
Father in Heaven and his Son, Jesus Christ,
The people who play by the book receive power from on High,
which can help all people at any time and in any place
to bring wonder and question to all who have an
interest in learning about the power of God.
If you receive some of this power,
do not misuse it or you will
have it taken away
faster than you can say no!

## HOW TO HEAL A BROKEN HEART

L. TALMAGE GORRINGE

When people receive broken hearts,
they find themselves alone,
so they mourn, 'til someone comes and delivers a
message of peace and happiness to their soul.
People understand a portion on how to keep a
Relationship alive and fresh,
'til they find something that they couldn't live with anymore,
then, one of them breaks off the relationship.
Our Father in Heaven helps us find good ways to mend hearts,
so neither one of us will hold on to the pain of braking up
and becoming enemies.
You have to have faith in our Father in Heaven
that He will comfort your heart and give you
wisdom to make a truce with one another.
and bring power unto your eternal sphere, *which is to come.*

# THE USUAL AND THE UNUSUAL

L. TALMAGE GORRINGE

The usual are things that

can be seen by the naked eye.

you must have faith,

a will to live with God in the Highest,

(The Celestial kingdom), and must give your life if

necessary.

The unusual bringeth eternal happiness and love to

your eternal sphere.

The usual bringeth temporal pleasures to your mind

and body,

but in the long run, makes you sad and alone.

The unusual bringeth you close to God.

The people who can see

the unusual are righteous

And spiritual too.

Before you can see the unusual,

## NEVER KNOWN SUCH PAIN

L. TALMAGE GORRINGE

Never known such pain, that overwhelmed my body;
such anguish and terror I could not
make peace with my body and spirit, to learn from my mistakes,
to bring to my focus the eternal plan of misery and woe.
Never known such pain,
to try to make all my rights to wrongs,
and to bring me down where unto the devil lives.
Never known such pain, that Satan tempts me with,
to try to bring me down unto his level of misery and woe.

## I WILL BE THERE

L. TALMAGE GORRINGE

Sometimes it is hard to ask for help, because
we like to feel independent.
We may feel independent enough to turn people away, to give them a sense of
being unneeded, in things that we find hard to do.
When we need help,
we usually refuse,
and get more frustrated,
'til we break down and ask for help,
which is when we receive it.
The people who ask for help when needed,
are always willing to help others.
As we help others,
they will help us, without hesitation.

## NEVER KNOWN SUCH LOVE

### L. TALMAGE GORRINGE

Never known such love, that overwhelms
me from the top of my body to the bottom,
to give unto me peace and happiness to
my heart and soul,
so I may live the life that is pleasing to me and my
Father in Heaven and his Son, Jesus Christ,
(The Savior of the World).
Never known such love, that can
make me happy for eternity.
Never known such love, that a wife gives unto me
to remind me from time to time of
the eternal goals, which we have made.
Never known such love, that our
Father in Heaven and his Son, Jesus Christ, give unto me,
to bring me closer to them,
to keep me strong in the gospel of Jesus Christ,
and to help me become "One" with the Father.


## MASTERPIECE

### L. TALMAGE GORRINGE

Everyone has a masterpiece,
but few discover it.
Once you have discovered your personal masterpiece,
you've learned what you need to do to be
glorified to the Highest degree of glory, (The Celestial Kingdom).
When you've discovered your personal masterpiece,
you've received Christ's picture in your countenance.
To have a masterpiece is to find yourself, but first you must find Christ, the Lord.
When you've discovered your masterpiece, you are able to do all things.

# I CAN'T FIGHT THIS . . .

### L. TALMAGE GORRINGE

I can't fight this feeling anymore,
for ye are the one who I desire to have as my wife,
for all eternity.
I can't fight this feeling anymore,
for ye are the most beautiful person
I have the pleasure of meeting and getting to know.
People who can't control their feelings
usually find themselves getting in trouble.
I want to bring love to you, eternally.
People who can control their feelings,
are able to share them at the perfect time and place.

# TRUE HEARTS

### L. TALMAGE GORRINGE

True hearts are "One" with God;
they obey His will, and are eternally happy.
To bring love to all those who hearken to your words,
and receive the Holy Spirit in their lives.
True hearts are compassionate, and peaceful to be around;
they bring souls unto God,
and receive eternal happiness and great joy into their lives.
True hearts help those in need of someone to lean on,
to listen, or to help when needed.
True hearts are there when you need one,
to comfort in time of need.
True hearts are "True."

# HOLD ME

L. Talmage Gorringe

Hold me with the love which
your heart holds for God,
that ye may receive a Higher
Love from the One who loves you.
Hold me with the love that comes to you,
when you have discovered another
sacred principle of
the True and Everlasting Gospel of Jesus Christ,
to bring to you a greater understanding
of life on earth.
Hold me forever,
that ye may not loose the
love which your heart holds,
to take you to the place where you
are happy eternally.
Hold me 'til you no longer have
the strength to hold me.
Then,
I will hold you 'til we reach
the Celestial kingdom.

# SHOW YOUR TRUE COLORS

L. TALMAGE GORRINGE

Show your true colors,

which bringeth the best out of you,

to let people know that you can be trusted.

As you show your true colors,

you will find peace, happiness,

and great joy in your life.

Show your true colors,

that you may find your

eternal companion,

to dwell in happiness for eternity.

People who show their true colors,

are always happier and more aware of

the plan of holiness and salvation.

Show your true colors,

so you may receive power

unto the Kingdom of God.

As you show your true colors,

you will draw people unto you,

because of the way you live your life.

Show your true colors,

so you may have a great day every day.

# QUIET SOULS

L. Talmage Gorringe

People who have quiet souls,
find themselves afraid to show their true
feelings and emotions toward others.
People who are quiet in everything they do,
find peace in themselves,
but not in God or in the world;
they create a world for themselves
and let no one else enter their lives.
People who have quiet souls,
find themselves lost all the time,
no matter where they go or who they meet.
People who have quiet souls,
are scared to grow up and
learn how to succeed in life.
These people are ashamed
of something they have done,
which can keep them in a
realm of make-believe
and terror.

# THE FATHER I ALWAYS HAD BUT NEVER KNEW

## L. TALMAGE GORRINGE

*The Father I always had, but never knew*
He guides me with His shining light,
to bring me unto the truthfulness of His love.
I will learn to become more like my Father in Heaven;
He makes me happy when I feel of His presence.
*The Father I always had, but never knew*
He is righteous and spiritual too;
He is my teacher and my debtor;
He gives me peace to know that I will
live with my Father which art in Heaven for eternity.
He is my Father which lives in Heaven!
He is my Father which lives in Heaven.

## THE WILL OF THE HEART

### L. TALMAGE GORRINGE

The will of the heart shows courage.
The will of the heart stands up for what it believes in.
The will of the heart teaches the gospel of Jesus Christ.
The will of the heart is pure, and in tune with the promptings of God,
The Eternal Father.

## JOURNALS

### L. TALMAGE GORRINGE

Journals are our life written down on paper.
Journal show our enjoyable, sad, upsetting, and happy experiences.
Journals shows our past, present, and future periods of time.

# FAITH

L. TALMAGE GORRINGE

It takes faith to do the will of the Father.
Faith is believing in things which are not seen, but are true.
Faith is knowledge; knowledge is wisdom; wisdom is power.
Faith is knowing that you are doing the will of the Father.
Faith without works is dead.

## THE SCRIPTURES

L. TALMAGE GORRINGE

The scriptures bringeth souls unto
the knowledge of the plan of happiness;
it bring them closer to our
Father in Heaven and his Son, Jesus Christ.
If people read the scriptures daily,
they will find happiness in their lives for eternity.
The scriptures have the gospel of Jesus Christ in them.
The scriptures have the answers to life's questions.

## LIFE

L. TALMAGE GORRINGE

Life is like a box of chocolates,
you never know what you're going to bite into the next day.
Life can be predictable to one but not to another.
Life can be enjoyable or harsh.

## THE SOUL

L. TALMAGE GORRINGE

The soul is forever young.
The soul never lieth.
The soul receiveth love and peace into your heart and mind.
The soul bringeth truth to your heart and mind.
The soul never dies.

## DIRECTION

L. TALMAGE GORRINGE

The gospel will give you direction,
if you ask for it.
But the only way you will receive
direction is by a sincere heart,
and pondering of the soul,
and then pray unto the Father to find
out whether it is true or not and he will
answer you through the Holy Ghost

## JUDGE

L. TALMAGE GORRINGE

Judge not another person, for ye may judge him wrongly
if ye judge, ye will be judged, therefore, judge them not.
Judge rightly on the choices you make.

## ETERNAL LIFE

L. TALMAGE GORRINGE

Eternal life is living forever with our
Father in Heaven and his Son, Jesus Christ.
Eternal life is pure, peaceful, beautiful, and precious.
Eternal life is Holy and Glorious.
Eternal life is having the pure love of God always in your heart.
Eternal life is being clean on the great and glorious day of Exaltation.

## CLEANSE

L. TALMAGE GORRINGE

I had bathed to strip the dirt from my body,
so I can be cleansed spiritually through the power of God,
for I am not like our Father in Heaven;
for I am a little seed of our Father in Heaven;
for He has the power to cleanse my soul.

# RETURN WITH HONOR

### L. TALMAGE GORRINGE

Return with honor is living
the commandments and laws of God,
and enduring to the end.
He who returns with honor has the
love of God always in his heart;
he has done his best to do The Will of the Father.
He who returns with honor is prayerful
unto the Father with every decision he is faced with.
He who returns with honor is at peace with our Father.


# DAD

### L. TALMAGE GORRINGE

Dad has pure love for his children
Dad is a peacemaker
Dad is a great helper
Dad is a great grower, in spirit
Dad is tough when it
comes to problems in the household,
but gentle with everyone's feelings.
Dad is a dad.


# MOM

### L. TALMAGE GORRINGE

Mom has pure love for her children
Mom is a care keeper
Mom is a helpful person
Mom is a peaceful person to be around
Mom is gentle with every situation that she faces
Mom, you're the greatest
Mom is a mom

## I WILL FOLLOW THEE

L. TALMAGE GORRINGE

I will follow Thee until I am exalted.
I will follow Thee until I have a
perfect knowledge of Thee
and thy Son, Jesus Christ.
I will follow Thee until I am happy.
I will follow Thee until I have great joy in my soul.

## SPIRITUAL HEALTH

L. TALMAGE GORRINGE

He who has spiritual health has a great relationship
with our Father in Heaven and his Son, Jesus Christ.
Spiritual health is having the spirit of God
with you at all times and in all places.
He who has spiritual health knows the
will of the Father and obeys it.

## WISDOM

L. TALMAGE GORRINGE

Wisdom is having no doubt in what you know
wisdom is having the knowledge of good and evil
when you have the knowledge and
wisdom to help others in life, you are unstoppable.
Wisdom is a pure knowledge of a
portion of the gospel of Jesus Christ.
Wisdom is knowledge applied

## DEATH

L. TALMAGE GORRINGE

Death is part of our Heavenly Father's plan.
When you die, your body rests in peace
in the earth
to await the resurrection and redemption of the world,
to be judged by our Heavenly Father and his Son, Jesus Christ.
Death is a sad thing, but I know that I will be with my family for eternity.

# PRAYER

L. TALMAGE GORRINGE

Prayer is the way you communicate
to our Father in Heaven.
Prayer is powerful.
As you pray, pray with sincerity of heart,
wanting to know the Will of the Father.
As you pray,
pray with a broken heart and a contrite spirit.
Prayer takes faith that our Father in Heaven will answer you;
as you pray with faith, you will receive by faith.

# TURN YOUR HEART TO GOD

L. TALMAGE GORRINGE

Turn your heart to God, and you'll be happy forever.
Turn your heart to God, and He will guide you back to His presence.
Turn your heart to God, and He will show you where you can find peace.

# FAMILY

L. TALMAGE GORRINGE

Families are forever and eternal
Family unity shows love for each other
Friends can help friends become family
Friends are family
The circle of our family is forever and eternal
Family members can bring peace to other family members
Family members can make others feel happy and have a very enjoyable life

# WORK

L. TALMAGE GORRINGE

He who works listens and learns.
The people who work by the
spirit are closer to our Father in Heaven
and his Son, Jesus Christ.
The people who don't work by
the spirit are hard-hearted and refuse
to do the work of the Lord.
Work is a marvelous thing;
as you work, you grow closer
to our Father in Heaven and his
son, Jesus Christ.
Work is peaceful, pure, and precious.
Work without faith is dead.

# SUCCESS

L. TALMAGE GORRINGE

To have success you must achieve a certain level of spirituality
To have success you must strive for education, and never stop learning
To have success you must teach with the spirit
To have success you must stay on the
straight and narrow path which leads to eternal life with God.

# LISTEN

L. Talmage Gorringe

The people who listen to the prophet,
the promptings of the Holy Ghost, and to
the words of God and his Son, Jesus Christ
(The Savior of The World) are on the path to eternal life.
As you listen,
ponder what the Holy Ghost says to you
so you may find a way to make yourself
stronger than what you are now,
so you can grow closer to our
Father in Heaven and his Son, Jesus Christ,
to have a better understanding of the gospel of Jesus Christ.

# THE LOVE SECRET

L. Talmage Gorringe

The love secret
is having joy in your heart,
soul, and mind.
The love secret
is having peace in your heart,
mind, and soul.
The love secret
is sacred, true, and unconditional.
The love secret
comes from the heart,
soul, and mind.

## THE GRIEF OF LOVE

L. TALMAGE GORRINGE

The grief of love is looking at
pornographic pictures,
and naked people.
It is the desire to go against the will
of the Father, and fall into Satan's snares.
Try not to look at these things.
If ye obstain, ye will receive great understanding of the plan of
happiness and salvation,
which will lead you to the Highest degree of glory (The Celestial Kingdom).

## UTAH

L. TALMAGE GORRINGE

(MOUNTAIN ON HIGH)
Utah is the mountain on high that
bringeth you closer to our
Father in Heaven and his Son, Jesus Christ.
Utah is in the clouds where God and his Son, Jesus Christ dwell.
Utah is a peaceful place.
Utah is an inspired, historical land.

## THE ROSE

L. TALMAGE GORRINGE

I am a rose,
who grows big and strong
to bring love into the air for all to see,
for I am pretty and precious to look at.

## FEAR

L. TALMAGE GORRINGE

Fear without action is dead.
Fear is being alone.
Fear is being afraid that something
bad is going to happen to you or someone you love.
The only way you can overcome your fear is to face it.

# LOST

L. TALMAGE GORRINGE

When you feel lost,
you should go into a private place and
offer up a personal prayer unto our
Father in Heaven,
and He will help you find your way back.

# THE HIGHEST LOVE

L. TALMAGE GORRINGE

The Highest Love anyone can achieve
is the love that our Father in Heaven gives unto me.
The Highest Love is purer than the purest piece of gold
and brighter than the sun at it brightest.
The Highest Love is genuine, true,
and pleasurable above all other kinds of love.

# HEART FULL OF RAIN

L. TALMAGE GORRINGE

The heart full of rain has a determination
to live or die for what it believes in,
to proclaim the gospel of Jesus Christ to those who
will hearken to the words of God
the Eternal Father and his Son, Jesus Christ.
The heart full of rain comes from the soul,
to bring peace and happiness to all those
who hearken to Father's words.
The heart full of rain gives you love that
brightens all things,
to bring to you knowledge
and wisdom for the good of the world.

## ROYAL FAMILY

L. TALMAGE GORRINGE

The Royal Family cares, loves,
and enjoys each other's company.
The Royal Family is courteous,
kind, and true to the
commandments and laws of God.
The Royal Family is an example to
members and nonmembers alike.
The Royal Family teaches the
gospel of Jesus Christ to all
those who hearken to the servants
of God the Eternal Father.


## THE RIVER

L. TALMAGE GORRINGE

As I follow the river,
I should pray for guidance
from my Father in Heaven,
so He can bring me back to my family,
so we may be together forever.
I follow the river to pure waters,
so I may find my way back to the Father.
As I follow the iron rod,
I will be led to the river of pure water,
where I may partake and live forever
with my Father
which art in Heaven.

# PRIVACY

L. TALMAGE GORRINGE

Privacy will make you strong,
as you work out the confusion and frustration
of your heart and soul,
which will give you joy and happiness for eternity.
The privacy that people need is to be alone,
to think things through,
so they will have a clear, sharp mind,
to be able to make difficult decisions and choices.
If you allow privacy in your home,
you will have an eternal trust with your family.


# HONOR

L. TALMAGE GORRINGE

We should honor our father and mother,
for they gave unto us the gift of life;
let us honor our father and mother 'til the debt is paid.
as we follow our father and mother,
be thankful for what they have done for us,
for without them we are lost in the world.
We will follow our father and mother 'til we have
learned all that we need to be able to return to our
Father and Mother;
for it is glorious to live in their presence.
When we follow our Father and Mother,
we should thank them for their guidance and eternal love.
I am pleased to have a Father and Mother
to lead me back to their presence,
for they know what my trials are,
and are willing to help me overcome them.
Let us honor our Father and Mother,
for they love us and will
bless us through all eternity.

# THE SACRED JOURNEY

L. TALMAGE GORRINGE

The sacred journey is a personal journey;
to make one happy eternally.
The sacred journey is peaceful, pure, and
glorious in the end.
The sacred journey allows our Father in Heaven
into our lives to help us in times of need.
The sacred journey has a heart full of love within it.
While you are on your sacred journey,
you will see a light at the end of your journey,
and there will be someone waiting
to encircle you with
all that He has.

# THE LOVE LETTER

L. TALMAGE GORRINGE

The love letter is romantic,
passionate, and true.
The love letter is a feeling of concern.
The love letter gives eternal happiness
and joy to your heart and soul.
The love letter is unconditional
and gentle to the ear and heart.
The love letter is tearful,
prayerful, and peaceful.
The love letter: Ask me no questions
I'll tell you no lies.
He who loves sends letters to show
intimacy, romance and fair play.
Love is physical and product full.

# HARD RAIN

L. Talmage Gorringe

Hard rain is dangerous to be in.
Hard rain is interesting to watch and listen to.
Hard rain hurts, if you have to be out in it.
Hard rain is good to have,
so the world can survive
a little while longer.
Hard rain comes from the clouds,
and releases big drops
of water to give nourishment
to all living things.
Hard rain has a sense of beauty but
only a few can identify it.
Everyone should feel hard rain
just to experience it once.


# TRUTH ETERNAL

L. Talmage Gorringe

To show truth, you need faith
that God our Father
will give us the knowledge
to prove something.
To receive truth eternal,
you must trust in God,
and listen for the truth that
He sends to your heart and soul.
To have the truth eternal of the plan of happiness,
You must listen to the *still small voice*
and act upon its promptings.

## STRIPLING WARRIORS

### L. TALMAGE GORRINGE

The Stripling Warriors stand strong in the church of God,
to build Zion for all the
world to watch, and then discover who we are.
The Stripling Warriors will fight to protect their families,
friends, religion, property, and
to keep everyone safe.
We are the Stripling Warriors,
who die fighting to protect "the family."
For those who die in their beliefs,
glory Shall be their reward, glory shall be their reward.

## THE PRIESTHOOD

### L. TALMAGE GORRINGE

The Priesthood is able to see all things,
if it is in
accordance with the Father.
All men are able to hold the keys of the priesthood
and exercise them in a manner that will bring
eternal life and exaltation to him and all he comes in contact with, that all may
dwell with God for eternity.
I love holding and exercising the Priesthood;
because it brings me closer to
God the Father and his Son, Jesus Christ, to receive eternal life and
dwell with them for all eternity.
The Priesthood keeps me alive
'til I am able to accomplish
the journey on which He has sent me.
The power of the Priesthood is incredible,
it can bring a sick person to health,
a blind man to see,
and raise a man from the dead
to let all the world see
what power and authority
God has over us.

# THE FALL OF ADAM

### L. TALMAGE GORRINGE

We, as members of
The Church of Jesus Christ
Of Latter-day Saints,
do not look
upon the
fall of Adam
as the cause of sin
in the world;
we look upon
the Fall of Adam
as a blessing
that we may be able
to return to our
Father's presence,
to dwell with Him forever.
As I live
in accordance to the laws of God,
I find that Adam fell that
men might be,
and men are that they might have joy;
for without Adam to transgress
and fall,
we would not be.
Therefore, it is a blessing that
he fell for me to live.
As I live, I love, and as I love, I find,
and as I find, I exalt, and as I exalt, I teach,
and as I teach, I learn, and as I learn, I receive,
and as I receive, I pray,
and as I pray, I become more like God the Father
and Jesus Christ.
The Fall of Adam
is a pure sacrifice unto all
who took the first estate and
are Now living
the second estate.

# LOVE vs. LOVE

### L. Talmage Gorringe

The love of man is an average lifestyle which gives you temporal blessings that will frustrate you and get you nowhere in the world today.

The love of man brings temporal happiness, romance, and unexalted relationships to your life, to bring you down into despair and woe, to
live in misery forever.

The love of man gives imperfection to his soul by not looking at the whole picture, and taking in only the things that please the mind temporally and non-existently.

When people don't communicate with love and affection, they tend to grow apart and become enemies to one another, to hate each other and never talk kind words to one another again.

The love of man will only get you as far as the Telestial kingdom, which is the glory of the stars.
The love of God is pure, eternal, and inviting to all those who hearken to His voice.

The love of God bringeth eternal and spiritual happiness to your heart and soul, which gives me a greater light and knowledge of the plan of happiness to be perfect always.

The love of God is perfect love and enjoyable for others to feel and
contemplate, to bring to you a peace of eternal life, with God.

When people communicate with love and affection, they are creating
a friendship that will last eternally.

The love of God will lead you to the Celestial kingdom, which is the highest of all kingdoms, to dwell with God for eternity

# TAKE ME HOME

### L. Talmage Gorringe

As I strive to reach my home,
I find trials and tribulations in my way,
to help me grow strong in the
gospel of the kingdom of God,
to bless me with
the blessings of the kingdom, to give unto me
the Power, and glory of God.
Take me home,
where God dwells;
keep me safe from
the things of the world;
bring perfection to
my loved ones and me
to dwell with God for eternity.
Take me home that I may feel of thy love,
bring peace to my heart and soul tonight
that I may receive
the kingdom of God and much much more.
Take me home
so I may dwell amongst my family
and live forever with God (The Father).
As I strive to reach my eternal home,
I find peace and humility to guide
me through the trials of life.
When I find my home on high,
I have the place where I will
dwell for eternity,
To bring perfection to my soul and
live forever in peace and
happiness for eternity.

## EXPRESSIVE SOUL

### L. Talmage Gorringe

The expressive soul invites you unto God,
so you may learn of the love,
determination, and mercy,
which God has for you;
to give unto them eternal life and exaltation;
like unto God.
He who loves God, loves himself and
has greatness in his heart,
to do the will of the Father,
and to find a way back to His presence,
to dwell with Him for eternity.
The expressive soul is peaceful,
pure, and controllable in the site of God and man;
and receives power and authority,
to have no fear.
God will protect you in your endeavors,
as you live a prosperous life.
He comes when there is danger,
opposition,
or when someone is in need of help.
The expressive soul takes
problems and gives them unto God,
so I may continue to do the will of the Father
and live forever in happiness.
The expressive soul is
forever young
and always there
when you are in need of
comfort.

# KNOWLEDGE

### L. TALMAGE GORRINGE

Knowledge is beautiful.
You can gain knowledge
by learning from your interest and expanding light of that specific interest.
Knowledge can become wisdom
by testifying and sharing your feelings
on what you know to be true and having confidence in what you are saying.
Knowledge can help you gain wisdom

# MARVELOUS MOMENTS

### L. TALMAGE GORRINGE

Marvelous moments are enjoyable to reflect on
the moments which people have are peaceful,
pure, and inviting,
to give them happiness in their heart and soul,
and to bring love to all that know them.
Marvelous moments are exciting, fun,
and memorable to oneself,
to bring exaltation
to your loved ones and you.
Marvelous moments are marvelous.

# CHURCH

### L. TALMAGE GORRINGE

The Church of Jesus Christ of Latter-day Saints
is the only true church upon the face of this land,
whereby the fullness of the gospel of Jesus Christ
and the mysteries of Heaven are unfolded within it.
This church is led by Jesus Christ
(The Savior of the World,) through revelation,
and through prophets called of God.
This gospel will bring you happiness
through the eyes of our Father in Heaven and
His Son, Jesus Christ, by reading, pondering,
and praying unto the Father to find out if it is true or not.
The principles and ordinances of the gospel
are true and beautiful.

# PATIENCE

L. TALMAGE GORRINGE

Being patient is being at peace with yourself and others
Being patient brings great joy into your life
Patience brings happiness into your heart
Patience brings love to your loved ones and you
Being patient is attractive
Being patient is of the essence
Patience is being kind without hurting or bothering others
Those who have patience are courteous towards others
Patience can show calmness
Patience is wonderful

# TRUE FRIENDS

L. TALMAGE GORRINGE

True friends help resolve concerns,
and they are always there when you need them.
True friends loves to have fun;
true friends are gentle with your feelings,
and love to make you feel good.

# REMEMBRANCE

L. TALMAGE GORRINGE

Remember there is only
one way to return to Heavenly Father's presence:
through Christ Jesus (The Savior of the world).
Remember that our Father in Heaven
and Jesus Christ live and want
us to strive to come back unto their presence.

# TEARS OF THE WORLD

L. TALMAGE GORRINGE

The tears of the world are many.
Tears shed are precious;
they help you express your feelings towards others;
it shows someone you care about him,
and are going to miss him.
Tears spread are pure and precious.
As you shed tears, your heart
softens to people's feelings
so you may understand
a greater portion of what the person.
Is trying to say.

# A FACE IN A CROWD

L. TALMAGE GORRINGE

A face in a crowd is in a group,
wherefore the face that isn't in the crowd is alone.
He who is alone has no friends,
and needs to make some friends.
He who is alone,
needs to pray unto our Father above
for help in finding new friends,
and he will help you.
A face in a crowd is one of
our Father in Heaven's children.
Heavenly Father loves and cares about that face dearly,
and wants to rescue from the temptations of the world.
A face in a crowd is so rebellious
and proud to be Mine,
to nourish and love forever and ever.
A face in a crowd is pure,
peaceful, and precious to look at.


# HUMILITY

L. TALMAGE GORRINGE

Humility is humbling yourself before God.
When you show humility, you are showing meekness unto God.
Humility is showing patience and long
suffering unto God The Almighty, to give thanks,
and to be in tune with the spirit of truth.
Being humble is being at peace with yourself
and with God, to act according to His Will.
To have humility you must first be
patient, meek, and submissive;
Then you will have humility in your heart.


# TESTIMONY

L. TALMAGE GORRINGE

As you testify of what you know to be true,
your testimony will grow stronger and stronger.
As you testify,
you show your love toward others;
and you may give unto them a desire to learn more.
Testimonies build character.
Testimonies bring you closer to
the knowledge of our Father in Heaven.

# BLESSINGS

L. TALMAGE GORRINGE

You can feel blessings in your heart and soul.
Blessings make you happy and bring you close
to our Father in Heaven and his Son, Jesus Christ.
Blessings bringeth peace to your heart and soul.
Blessings make you humble and honest.

# AM I

L. TALMAGE GORRINGE

Am I strong, and able to overcome
the temptations of the Evil One?
Am I doing what the Lord, Jesus Christ, wants
me to do?
Is my heart at peace with my mind,
and with our Father in Heaven and his Son, Jesus Christ?

# MISSIONARIES

L. TALMAGE GORRINGE

Missionaries are here to bring souls unto repentance,
to instill the knowledge of Heavenly Father and
His Son, Jesus Christ, and provide the plan of happiness.
Missionaries are spiritually on an incline,
feeling the spirit of the Lord, Jesus Christ, at all times and in all places.

# RIGHTEOUS

L. TALMAGE GORRINGE

He who is righteous,
is spiritual too
and is close to our
Father in Heaven
and his Son, Jesus Christ.
He who is righteous,
keeps the commandments of God,
the Eternal Father.

# TELESTIAL BODY

L. Talmage Gorringe

The Telestial Body is for those people who look at life temporally,
and not eternally, to give them Temporal happiness,
and think that there is no increase after this life;
where in fact, there is increase and there is not
enough comprehension to understand
fully why these people don't receive an increase in their lives.
The Telestial Body is like unto the stars.

# TERRESTIAL BODY

L. Talmage Gorringe

The Terrestial body is for those people
who will keep half of the commandments and laws of God;
to bring them unto the knowledge of the Terrestial Kingdom,
and be able to dwell with Jesus Christ,
(The Savior of the world)
for eternity.
The Terrestial body is like unto the moon.

# CELESTIAL BODY

L. Talmage Gorringe

The Celestial body is for those people
who strive to keep all the commandments and laws of God,
to bring unto them an eternal increase,
and to be exalted to the highest kingdom,
to dwell with God
(The Eternal Father)
And his Son, Jesus Christ
(The Savior of the world).
The Celestial body is like unto the sun.

# BLIND PEOPLE

L. Talmage Gorringe

The people who are blind to the truth
are not in tune with the spirit of the Lord, Jesus Christ.
The people who are blind
are unfaithful to the promptings of the Lord, Jesus Christ.
As you study and pray about the
scriptures, you should ask God
in the name of Jesus Christ
for help and guidance.

# HEART AND SOUL

L. TALMAGE GORRINGE

Home is where "the heart" of
the family begins.
When I see you, my heart
goes out to
please
you.
You make my heart
sing with joy.
When I see your eyes,
my heart
cries for you.
When I am with you,
my heart goes out to you.
When I am with you,
you make me feel
like I am with the girl of my dreams.
When I see you
my heart and soul would do anything for you.
When I see you, you make me fall
to my knees in front of you,
to please you in everything of everyday.
"Home is where the heart is."

# PROBLEMS

L. TALMAGE GORRINGE

As you receive problems by some unwise act,
you should turn your problems over to the Lord
so he may guide you through it,
and have you learn from it,
so you won't make the same mistake again.
When you receive a problem
by some other means, you ought not waste any time
but resolve that problem as soon as possible.
If you let the problem linger for a long period of time,
you are letting the problem grow bigger and bigger
until you can no longer
take care of it by yourself, so take care of it quickly.
When you do receive a problem or two,
act quickly so the Lord may bless you
for acting and responding quickly to the problem.
Problems help you grow so you may become a better person.

# MORNING

L. TALMAGE GORRINGE

Without mornings
there are no nights.
You can have
a great day,
if you desire
to have
one.
Mornings
are peaceful.
Mornings can start you off
on the right foot,
so you can have
a great day.

# FOG

L. TALMAGE GORRINGE

Fog is clouds that
come close to the earth.
Fog can be thick or thin.
Fog can become
humid.
Some people don't like the fog
because it makes it hard for them
to see in front of their faces.
Fog is part of nature.

# OCEANS

L. TALMAGE GORRINGE

Oceans are peaceful,
pure,
and romantic to listen to and play in.
I love the sounds of
the ocean because I feel at peace with the Father,
and I feel that I can do anything.
Oceans are sophisticated,
and pretty to listen to as well.
Oceans are natural bodies of water.
Oceans are fun to play in.

# SHADE

Shade is where
the sun doesn't shine.
Shade is natural,
calm, cool, and dark.
Shade is peaceful,
romantic, and a pure delight.
Shade saves me from getting heatstroke.
Shade is a marvelous,
natural thing.


# FOUNTAINS

L. TALMAGE GORRINGE

There are water fountains,
fountains of youth,
fountains of pure water,
and drinking fountains.
Water fountains are pretty
and precious to look at and desire.
The fountain of youth makes you look
and feel younger than
you really are.
There are fountains of pure water,
to strip yourself
from the dirt
and sin of the world.
There are drinking fountains
that you may get
a drink from.


# ROADS OF MISERY AND WOE

L. TALMAGE GORRINGE

The roads not taken, are those that
involve gangs,
drugs,
People who drink and smoke,
and like to
destroy their bodies by
having intercourse
with others;
these are the roads
that can steer
a life to become
murderers in the home,
with hardly any money to live,
and wear clothes that have
been thrashed and rethrashed.


46

# CHARACTER

L. TALMAGE GORRINGE

He who has character is fun to be with.
Everyone has character, just some show it more than others.
Some with less character might get you in trouble, just to save their butt.

# SUN

L. TALMAGE GORRINGE

The sun helps plants grow.
If plants get the right amount of sunlight,
they will grow big and strong to survive the cold winters.
The sunlight cannot soley help a plant grow;
it needs some
help from water.
The sun is a marvelous thing;
it can keep us from getting cold,
and we can have fun in the sun.

# DANCERS

L. TALMAGE GORRINGE

The people who love to dance
have many methods and styles of dancing.
The people who dance are having fun.
Dancers show
different styles of dancing,
and they do it beautifully.
They have unique, unseen moves
that only dancers can recognize.
Dancers are swift and pure.

# THE GREAT WATERS

L. TALMAGE GORRINGE

The great waters
will lead you
to the
promised land
where there are no
lustful thoughts
or feelings abiding;
but the only way you will know if it
is the Promised land,
is by your spirituality
your personal righteousness,
and your relationship with
our Father in Heaven.
The great waters will lead you to
the choicest land,
Above all other lands.

# A GENTLE WIND

L. TALMAGE GORRINGE

A gentle wind which takes away the dreadful heat of the sun, blows to calm
the aching body.
The gentle wind is not my enemy; it helps me stay cool when I get too hot.
The gentle wind is peaceful, pure, and ongoing.

# ORCHIDS

L. TALMAGE GORRINGE

Orchids are pretty and precious to look at.
Orchids are as easy as one, two, three, to grow.
Therefore, the people who grow orchids
are willing to try new things,
they are willing to try to grow an orchid.
There are many
different kinds of orchids,
with many
unique names.

# RAINY DAYS

L. TALMAGE GORRINGE

The people who have rainy days
may be very gloomy;
there are
those who don't want to do anything fun
with their friends or family;
they just want to read,
watch the rain, or ponder.
Rainy days are dark and dreary;
therefore,
it is very comfortable.

# BEAUTY

L. TALMAGE GORRINGE

There are many ways you can find beauty.
Beauty can be found in the desert, mountains, animals, and people.
Beauty is everywhere.
Beauty can be destroyed if we don't take care of it.
Please preserve the beauty.

# SLIP

L. TALMAGE GORRINGE

You can slip
in many places;
when a surface is wet,
you can slip
all over the place,
so be careful
with wet surfaces.
Snow and ice can also be slippery,
so be careful.
Slipping and sliding can be fun;
it can also be dangerous,
so play it safe.

# SCARS

L. TALMAGE GORRINGE

Scars are painful.
The scars that show
on physical bodies
are sometimes
painful to talk about.
The mental scars are hard to
get rid of,
but easy to hide; they can destroy your life,
because you won't let anybody into your life,
so you may begin to have fun again.

# WHAT IF . . .

L. TALMAGE GORRINGE

What if I wasn't LDS?
What would I do or become?
What if I knew not who I was?
What if I didn't serve an LDS mission?
What if my marriage isn't an eternal marriage?
What if I can't support myself or my family?
What if I'm not a good husband?
Will I have fallen into Satan's trap?

# TRAITS

L. TALMAGE GORRINGE

Traits are inherited from your parents.
There are good and bad traits,
the bad traits will get you in trouble,
so dump them, and keep the good traits;
use them wisely.

# MOCKERY

L. TALMAGE GORRINGE

Mockery is of the devil;
mockery is around every corner;
mockery makes you weak;
try not to mock your friends;
and you will be better off.

# WHEN A MAN MARRIES A WIFE

L. TALMAGE GORRINGE

When a man takes a wife,
the man will find
her weaknesses
and help her
make them strengths.
When a woman takes a husband,
she will find
his weaknesses
and help him make
them strengths.
When a woman takes a husband,
she will find out about
his eternal goals,
so they can strive
for the same goals
at the same time,
and then, they can
help each other out.

# O MY FRIENDS

L. TALMAGE GORRINGE

O, my friends, who walk in the shadow of my footsteps
O, my friends, who are always there when I need them
O, my friends, who support me in everything I do
O, my friends, who help me when I need help

# WHO AM I

L. TALMAGE GORRINGE

Who am I?
I am a child of God.
I wonder what I am supposed to do?
Where am I supposed to go?
Where am I going?
Who am I going to meet?

# THE WIND SINGS

L. TALMAGE GORRINGE

The wind sings with
pure intent
to warn the people of the danger.
The wind sings gentle songs.
The wind sings with calmness.
The wind sings for people.
The wind sings.

# WHEN LIFE GETS HARD, KNEEL AND PRAY

L. TALMAGE GORRINGE

When life gets hard,
pray with real intent and a sincere heart.
As you pray, you are becoming like
our Father in Heaven and his
Son, Jesus Christ,
and you will be brought into
His sphere.

# FREEDOM

L. TALMAGE GORRINGE

We all have the freedom to choose good or evil.
If we choose evil, we will pay the consequences.
With our choices, we may be condemning ourselves to be with the Devil.

# FUN

L. TALMAGE GORRINGE

You can have fun and be serious at the same time.
You can have fun giving a discussion or giving a lesson
to someone and still learn something.
You can never have too much fun.

# SECRETS

L. TALMAGE GORRINGE

Secrets are sometimes
good not shared.
Secrets are gossip kept
from one person to another person.
Therefore, don't keep secrets.
Secrets are evil and are from the Devil.

# THE CHRISTMAS SPIRIT

L. TALMAGE GORRINGE

The Christmas Spirit is sharing
your presence with someone less fortunate.
The Christmas Spirit is peaceful, pure, and inviting.
Christmas is when we celebrate the birth of Christ, Jesus.

# PEOPLE

L. TALMAGE GORRINGE

Many people
love and care about you.
These people are
gentle with your feelings
and like to help you
keep your eternal
temple covenants with God
(The Eternal Father).

# UNCONDITIONAL LOVE

L. TALMAGE GORRINGE

Unconditional love is the
love of God
and his Son, Jesus Christ.
unconditional love is eternal
and exalted.
God, The Father, and Jesus Christ
have unconditional love
for everyone.
We too can have
unconditional love towards everyone.
Unconditional love is having
the spirit of God
with you at all times,
and in all things, and in all places,
acting upon the promptings of the Holy Spirit.

# THE GREAT LESSON

L. TALMAGE GORRINGE

The great lesson is peaceful,
pure, and unconditional;
to learn of
our Father in Heaven
and his Son, Jesus Christ.
You may know
of their will
and strive to
accomplish it,
and in return
you will have eternal life.
The great lesson will give you happiness
and great joy in your heart
so you can be convinced to choose the right.

# CHARITY

L. TALMAGE GORRINGE

Charity is everlasting love and care.
Charity is the pure love of God.
When you have charity, you can
do all things according to
the Will of the Father.
Charity suffereth long
and is kind.

# TRUST ME

L. TALMAGE GORRINGE

Trust me to do
the will of the Father.
Trust me that
I will be a good father
to my wife
and children.
Trust the Father to bless you
with the blessings
that will bring you to perfection,
like unto our Father.
Trust me that
I will treat you with respect.
Trust me that
I will help you resolve your problems.
Trust me that I will bring
peace and happiness to your heart and soul.

# POISON

L. TALMAGE GORRINGE

This poison will kill,
if you take it continually;
it will eat your body,
and your body won't function properly.
this poison;
Satan has power over
it will bring you down
into despair,
and you will be
miserable forever.
The poison will trap your mind,
so you will be subjected to
Satan and his power,
to live miserably in
Outer Darkness with him.
But: the poison is removable,
if you turn your heart to God, the Eternal Father
and allow him to lift
the poison from your body,
you will be healed.

# STARS

L. TALMAGE GORRINGE

As you look at the stars,
you are looking
into the midst of Heaven;
you are seeing all of
God's creations, which
he gloriously made for us
to admire and use as needed.
As I think of what the Father has done for me,
he has given unto me
the breath of life,
His only son,
and a world to beautify
and replenish the Celestial kingdom.
As I feel the presence of the Father, the Eternal Father,
He has given me the guidance
I need to return
back to him in glory
and in
great pleasure.

# ETERNAL VISION

L. TALMAGE GORRINGE

He who has the eternal vision, knows our Father personally and obeys Him.
He who has the eternal vision is at peace with our Father in Heaven and his Son, Jesus Christ.
He who has the eternal vision is in tune with the spirit of the Lord.
He who has the eternal vision can stop mistakes before they happen.

# RESPOND

L. TALMAGE GORRINGE

He who responds to the still small voice
is more knowledgeable to respond rather than reject.
He who responds to the still small voice becomes
closer to our Father in Heaven and his Son, Jesus Christ.
He who responds to the still small voice,
is at peace with our Father in Heaven and his Son, Jesus Christ.

# THE GARDEN

L. TALMAGE GORRINGE

The flower garden is pretty and precious to look at.
The garden shows you how precious,
pure, and fragile the flowers are;
It also shows you that you too can be
beautiful, physically and spiritually.

# WHEN I WOKE

L. TALMAGE GORRINGE

When I woke,
my life was put in order for me,
so I can learn
how to return back to
our Father in Heaven and his Son, Jesus Christ.
When I woke, I could feel the spirit
of the Lord more abundantly upon me, than ever before.
When I woke, it brought me closer
to our Father in Heaven and his Son, Jesus Christ.
When I woke, I made peace with my Father
and his Son, Jesus Christ.

# JESUS CHRIST

L. TALMAGE GORRINGE

He is Omega and Omnipotent;
He is my Savior
and Redeemer;
He is Jesus Christ,
who suffered for all mankind.
He is Jesus Christ,
the Son of the living God.
He is Jesus Christ,
the teacher and mediator of the world.
He is Jesus Christ, who does the will of the Father;
Jesus Christ knows each and every one of us, personally.
He knows what I'm going to do before I do it.
He gives me the plan of happiness,
that I may follow it and return
to our Father,
when the time cometh.

# FEELINGS

L. TALMAGE GORRINGE

Some of the feelings people have are
happy, sad, and angry.
They stir up confusion,
which causes contention against one another.
Feelings are emotional.

# THOUGHTS

### L. Talmage Gorringe

Thoughts can be dangerous.
If you are having thoughts
about committing sin,
you've already committed a
sin in your heart.
Thoughts can bear you up or
drag you down.
If you are having good thoughts,
you are free of sin.
If you have good thoughts,
they are from our Father in Heaven;
but bad thoughts,
are from the Devil.

# TEMPLES

### L. Talmage Gorringe

Temples are holy buildings
that have
the spirit of the Lord Jesus Christ
in them.
The people who go to the Temple must
be worthy
and clean to attend.
The people who go to the Temple,
make and perform sacred ordinances and
covenants with the Lord Jesus Christ
(The Savior of The World),
so they may be able
to live again
with our Father
and his Son,
Jesus Christ again.

# DATING

L. TALMAGE GORRINGE

Dating has the pure intent: to make
friends and to find an eternal
companion to marry in
God's Temple.
Blind dates can be scary,
but it usually turns out great.
Dating can be romantic,
fun
or challenging.


# MISSION PRESIDENTS

L. TALMAGE GORRINGE

Mission Presidents are faithful
in keeping the commandments
and laws of God,
to the best of their abilities.
Mission Presidents are peacemakers.
Mission Presidents love
the gospel of
Jesus Christ,
and love to share it with others.
Mission Presidents are called of God
to make sure the work
is going forth boldly, nobly, and independent.
Mission Presidents teach
the gospel of Jesus Christ
to the missionaries,
so the missionaries can teach
the gospel of Jesus Christ
to their investigators.
Mission Presidents speak
to apostles of God.
Mission Presidents are physical guides
for the missionaries
in the mission field.
Mission Presidents are in tune with
the spirit
of revelation and prophecy.
Mission Presidents help you succeed
in bringing the gospel of Jesus Christ to every ear.

# THE NOBLE AND GREAT ONES

### L. Talmage Gorringe

The Noble and Great Ones are on a spiritual incline,

to do the Will of the Father, and

to live in His presence for eternity.

As we grow and become the true and everlasting

noble and great ones,

we are becoming perfect,

like unto God our Father, who is perfect.

The Noble and Great Ones,

are those who discover the meaning of life,

and strive to accomplish their divine destiny,

which comes from God the Father,

to bless the lives of others and bring salvation,

and eternal life.

We are the Noble and Great Ones,

for in latter days,

we come to a better understanding of the plan of eternal life;

to bring eternal life to those who hearken

and watch how we live.

As we become the true Noble and Great Ones,

we begin to see and understand how

the Lord our God works and performs His plan,

in behalf of all of us,

in returning to Him.

# HOME TEACHERS/VISITING TEACHERS

L. TALMAGE GORRINGE

Home Teachers are messengers called by God, to help members and nonmembers, when needed or prompted by the Holy Ghost so no harm or accident will come upon them; to keep them on the straight and Narrow path, which leads to Eternal life.

As Home Teachers teach, they become closer to God the Father and his Son, Jesus the Christ, to bring a message from God on how to live better, more prosperous lives in this world and the world to come.

As you teach, you are taught, as you are taught, you grow,

as you grow, you become, as you Become, you receive, as you Receive, you are exalted.

Home Teachers are good friends to all.

Visiting Teachers are messengers called by God to teach all the truths of the gospel of Jesus Christ so they may have the opportunity to come unto God through the name of Jesus Christ, who suffered for us that we might not suffer in the sight of God.

Visiting Teachers are concerned about you and your happiness, to bring to you eternal life if you desire to receive it.

As we teach, we are taught, as we are taught, we receive, as we receive, we give, as we give, we become, as we become, we are exalted.

Visiting Teachers are good friends to all.

# FAST OFFERINGS

L. TALMAGE GORRINGE

Fast Offerings are charity funds
used to help those who are
suffering financially and
to support families in need.
Fast Offerings show love towards others.
Fast Offerings are pleasing to the soul,
and unto the Lord Jesus Christ.
As you give Fast Offerings,
you are giving the greatest gift of all,
the gift love and compassion.
As people pay Fast Offerings,
they are starting to understand how
the Lord Jesus Christ cares for all people.
As you pay Fast Offerings,
you receive a greater portion of the Lord Jesus Christ's
love in your heart and soul, to share to all.
Fast Offerings bring us closer to
the Father and his Son, Jesus Christ.

# TITHING

L. TALMAGE GORRINGE

Tithing is a precious thing,
with which the Lord has blessed us,
to meet the needs of members,
that they may live a prosperous life as well.
As we pay our Tithing,
we are paying off a portion of the debt
which Christ the Lord paid,
that we may not suffer the pains of the world, like unto the Lord.
Tithing is a precious way, whereon we may become closer to our Father, and
become perfect as He is.
We all took a portion of our Father's life with us,
when we came to earth
to learn and to exalt our bodies to the Celestial Kingdom,
the highest kingdom of all kingdoms.

# THE ETERNAL FAMILY

L. TALMAGE GORRINGE

The eternal family beautifies and replenishes the earth,
to live in a clean and prosperous land,
to abide by the laws and commandments of God,
to bring eternal life to all those who hearken to the word of God.
The eternal family must be married in God's kingdom to
receive the full blessings of having an eternal family.
We as parents have a sacred obligation to teach our
children the gospel of Jesus Christ,
He who suffered for us that we might not suffered.
As we form an eternal family,
we are creating like unto none other,
A world of peace, love, and compassion to all people,
to give them opportunities to
receive eternal life.
The eternal family is always obeying the will of the father,
and teaching others the truth.
As we become eternal families, we are able to see how God
performs through the priesthood, that we might understand
how strong the authority and power
of the priesthood actually is,
so one day we may have the opportunity to
perform the fullness of the holy priesthood,
and continue in it.
The eternal family is exalted to the highest degree of glory,
and the purest land, above all other lands, to beautify and
replenish for the good of our eternal family.

# MISSIONS

L. TALMAGE GORRINGE

Missions are spiritually uplifting;
they bring you to
the knowledge of the truth,
of the gospel of Jesus Christ,
they bring unto you a
personal love for the Savior.
Missions are dedicated to serve
our
Father
to bring souls back into His fold,
and to give all glory to Him.
Good tidings
will come as you serve
the Father and gain a better understanding
of the gospel of Jesus Christ.
The mission teaches you how
to set Eternal Goals.

# WORKING HANDS\WORKING HEARTS

## L. Talmage Gorringe

Working hands are in accordance with the commandments and laws of God, whereby they never cease to do the Will of God, or fail to obey the Will of the Father.

As you work with your hands, you are understanding a portion of how God works in keeping us in His fold, that we may be able to return to Him in power and glory, to dwell with Him for all eternity.

Working hands are swift and always in the sight of God, to be judged accordingly for their transgressions, that they may learn and overcome the snares of the world.

As you work with your hands, you are pleasing the people with whom you work for. "From them to you, all things are done."

Working hands are peaceful, pure, and unconditional to God and the world, where they can help receive eternal happiness and eternal love in their lives.

Working hearts are spiritual and willing to change the hearts of evil to good, that they may hear the word of God and be born again with the Spirit of God.

As you work your hearts to become more righteous in the sight of God, you become a teacher to teach others the way back to our Father's presence, to bring exaltation to their souls.

Working hearts allow room for love to enter in and soften the hearts of others, that they may receive a portion of eternal happiness and glory, like unto our Father.

As you work your heart, you receive a greater portion of knowledge and wisdom, which will help you lead your life back to our Father, and live forever in happiness.

Working hearts can change an evil person to good, and live forever in peace and happiness.

# THE WILL OF THE FATHER

L. Talmage Gorringe

The will of the Father is true and everlasting;

it brings happiness, peace, and eternal life to all

mankind.

Spiritual promptings can guide you back to our Father's

presence

to dwell in happiness for all eternity.

The will of the Father is pure, peaceful,

and unconditional

unto the Will of the heart,

to bring exaltation and eternal life to the soul.

As we hearken to the will of the Father,

we understand more fully how the Father

can make us perfect,

like unto Himself.

# WE'LL NEVER PART AGAIN

L. TALMAGE GORRINGE

We'll never part from the word of God,
for we as members of the kingdom of God,
are strong and faithful unto
God the Father
and his Son, Jesus Christ,
to bring peace and joy to our souls.
As we strive to stay close to the family,
we become united with pure hearts and souls,
that we may never part from the family again.
As we keep ourselves away from
the temptations of the world,
we become strong in the family, church,
and the pursuit of happiness and joy,
through the mediator of our lives.
We'll never part from the truth,
family, and the church again,
for we are able to resolve
all problems peacefully,
which makes us strong,
and close to
the Father.

# THE WINDOWS OF HEAVEN

### L. TALMAGE GORRINGE

The windows of Heaven are holes in the sky,
where angels and
servants are dwelling on high, watching us
progress to the Celestial Kingdom,
yea, and if ye are in trouble
they will come and help you out, that you may dwell in happiness for eternity.
These windows are visible to us if we are living rightiously.
Sometimes we can see these windows.
As we watch for these special times in our lives,
we will understand a greater deal of
the Plan of Happiness.

## HOLD ON

### L. TALMAGE GORRINGE

Hold on to dear life, and you will be happy for eternity,
lest ye fall into Satan's snares and be corrupted, to be in his power for eternity.
As you hold on and find your potential in life,
"you will be blessed to the ends of the earth" and receive eternal happiness forever and ever.
Hold on to the "Iron Rod" and everything will fall into place,
that you may dwell in happiness for eternity.
As ye hold on and keep the commandments of the Lord, Jesus Christ,
you will receive exaltation and eternal life, to dwell with our Father for eternity.
If you hold on and endure to the end,
you will inherit the Kingdom of our Father.

## THE LIGHT OF THE WORLD

### L. TALMAGE GORRINGE

People who have the light of the world,
have a good understanding of
where they're going and what they're destiny is in this life.
We are the light of the world,
for we understand a greater portion of
the Plan of Salvation,
which leads us to the greatest place on earth (The Celestial Kingdom).
The light of the world is brighter than the sun at noonday;
therefore, we ought not to be condemners of ourselves and others,
but that we ought to be partakers of Eternal Life and
the Celestial World.


## TOUCH THE HEAVENS

### L. TALMAGE GORRINGE

Touch the Heavens wherein no one can go without the help of our Father.
Touch the Heavens wherein you can find
happiness to your heart and soul,
which will lead you to perfection and eternal life with our Father.
As you touch the Heavens, you are seeing the kingdom of our Father,
wherefore, ye can comprehend
a greater portion of the plan of happiness, which is love eternal.
We can see how our Father loves us so much
that He gave his Only Begotten Son to die on the cross
at Golgotha to pay for our sins
so we may not suffer and die
a lonely,
painful death.

# FAITH IS STRONGER THAN SIGHT

## L. TALMAGE GORRINGE

Faith is stronger than sight;
without faith there is no hope,
and without hope there is no light,
hence, ye are struck dumb and lifeless.
As your faith groweth,
you begin to see the mysteries of God unfold to you,
to bring a greater understanding of the plan of happiness and salvation
to your heart and soul.
Without faith, can ye see the mysteries of Heaven? I say unto you, Nay, ye cannot.
People say, "Faith can move mountains", why canst not thou?
Faith suffereth long
and is kind unto
the soul.


# KINGDOM

## L. TALMAGE GORRINGE

What is a kingdom?
A kingdom is a place where ye can go to find peace, happiness,
and the pure love of our Father, which art in Heaven.
To feel and experience
the pure and eternal love,
which our Father gives unto us continually.
Therefore, we are made whole in our kingdom.
A kingdom bringeth life eternal and immortality
to all who understand
and give heed to this great
plan of happiness and salvation.

# THE REDEMPTION OF THE WORLD

## L. TALMAGE GORRINGE

The redemption of the world
cleanses you from sin, transgression,
and all evil that remains today.
The redemption of the world will be a cleansing by war and evil,
to purify the earth of all impurities and evil that exist in the world today.
The redemption of the world will be a glorious time in our lives to find out if we have been saved, in the
kingdom of our Father.


## A LOVER'S WAY

## L. TALMAGE GORRINGE

A lover's way is endless upon the clear blue sky,
to bring something so precious
it pierces the heart
and goes directly
to the soul,
to refine the fire of a lover.
The way to a woman's heart is through active listening,
understanding, and communicating,
which will give you a chance to learn about each other.
Lovers feel the breeze caressing their bodies
to give unto them a brief moment of
immortality and eternal life.
If you say what's in your heart,
you will find eternal life
to talk and experience the
everlasting love toward one another,
which will bring you closer to each other.

## TRUTH ETERNAL

### L. TALMAGE GORRINGE

To show truth,
you need faith that our Father in Heaven
will give us the knowledge
to prove the truth of it to someone.
To receive truth eternal,
you must trust in our Father,
and listen for the truth,
which He sends to your heart and soul.
To have truth eternal of the plan of happiness,
you must listen to the still small voice
and act upon its promptings.

## THE IRON ROD

### L. TALMAGE GORRINGE

The Iron Rod is the word of God,
which leads you to
eternal life.
As we stay hold to the Iron Rod,
we will grow strong in the church
and become perfect like unto God our Father.
We as children of God,
have covenanted with God the Father
that we will always remember Him and his Son, Jesus Christ,
and come unto Him for help, guidance, and personal growth,
that we may share our knowledge with our family and friends.
The Iron Rod is the word of God; wherefore,
never let go; if ye do,
ye will be lost.

## THE GARDEN OF EDEN

L. TALMAGE GORRINGE

The Garden of Eden is beautiful,
like unto the Kingdom of God; it has the spirit of God within it,
to bless and sanctify all who hearken to the will of the Father,
to be blessed by the Spirit and the Priesthood.
As we stay in the Garden of Eden,
we will be safe from the fiery darts of the adversary,
who wants us to be miserable for all eternity.
The Garden of Eden is held in our hearts
to keep us safe and on the straight and narrow path,
the Path that leads to eternal life with God.
This Garden holds all the power, glory,
and wisdom that will make us gods and goddesses
unto the most High God.

## THE LONE AND DREARY WORLD

L. TALMAGE GORRINGE

The Lone and Dreary World,
is where Satan dwells,
it is dark and dreary like unto himself,
he tempts the people of God to do evil and to turn away,
to turn to Satan, and dwell in pain and suffering.
This world is full of wickedness and confusion;
wherefore, ye must be careful,
for the good of your divine destiny, ye must be careful.
The Lone and Dreary World is Satan's world:
a world of pain and suffering like unto no other,
the most cruel, painful,
and miserable place you can ever dwell.

# ZION'S HILL

L. TALMAGE GORRINGE

Zion's Hill is glorious, like unto the Garden of Eden;
pure and peaceful in all it stands for,
it will bring to pass the immortality and eternal life of man,
to be exalted in the highest.
The people who live on Zion's Hill cannot be hit,
hence, a city sitting on a hill cannot be hit, and are saved;
therefore, set your life on a hill where Satan cannot dwell
or tempt ye to do evil,
for he lives in misery forever.
Zion's Hill is the hill of power,
glory, peace, and wisdom,
a place where God the Father visits often,
to help those souls who are
in need of wisdom and guidance.

# THE GRAPES OF WRATH

L. TALMAGE GORRINGE

The Grapes of Wrath are cunning, deceitful,
and persuasive to the souls who partake
and become trapped in the snares of the evil one,
who is Satan, The Devil.
The Grapes of Wrath, which Satan bringeth into our lives,
has no light in the kingdom of God,
it only has the power of darkness
which bringeth torture and pain to the heart and soul of mankind.
The Grapes of Wrath go
against all that our Father teaches,
and try to deceive us
by using our own weaknesses against us,
so we may fall into
despair and be miserable
for eternity, like unto himself.

## "BE ONE"

L. TALMAGE GORRINGE

Be One with God our Father,
like He is with his Son, Jesus Christ.
As you become One with the Father,
you gain a portion of eternal life,
which will help you make good decisions
on life's trials and tribulations.
Be One with the Father,
and you will dwell in power and glory.
As you are One with the Father,
you will be One with his Kingdom.

## THE ARMOR OF GOD

L. TALMAGE GORRINGE

The Armor of God is strong, true, and faithful to the Will of the Father.
As you put on the Armor of God,
you are putting your life in our Father's hands,
that He may guide you and direct you to the Celestial Kingdom,
to dwell with Him for eternity.
The Armor of God can kill off a nation with one terrible swift blow.
The armor of God is the power of the Priesthood, to bring to pass the
righteousness of His plan.
As you feast upon the words of the Father,
you are learning how to put on and use the Armor of God
for the good of all mankind, that you may see and to marvel at what the
Father will do for His children.
The Armor of God only works
when ye are righteous, faithful, and
work with the spirit.

# THE MIGHTY TRUMP

### L. TALMAGE GORRINGE

The Mighty Trump is sounding to every heart,
to call us unto repentance, for the Second Coming of the Lord, Jesus Christ, is nigh at hand,
to bring unto us Exaltation and Eternal life with God,
that we may live and be glorified by the Mighty hand of God, The Eternal Father and his
Son, Jesus Christ, The Savior of the world.
This Mighty Trump sounds to every heart,
that all may hearken and obey the warnings of the Second Coming.
The Mighty Trump sounds to warn us of that Second Coming; that is nigh at hand.

Prepare ye this day,
to see Christ The Lord.

# PERSONAL TEMPLES

### L. TALMAGE GORRINGE
## (BODIES)

Personal Temples are sacred, true, and private;
we reveal them only in proper places and to a select few.
These Temples always need nourishment;
without nourishment they won't function properly.
The way to one of these Temples is through love, kindness, faith, and peace;
without this you will not receive any Temple during your lifetime.
When you express your personal Temples, you reveal all things,
letting go of all the secrets which you've kept from other Temples
because you found or earned trust.

# THE MIGHTY CHANGE

## L. TALMAGE GORRINGE

The Mighty Change comes from within, and through the help of God;
we as God's children need this Mighty Change
to live in a manner that makes you and God happy.
The Mighty Change comes by means of
turning your heart from an unproductive life
to a healthy and Productive life,
like unto God's.
As we begin to see the Mighty Change,
we are intrigued that we were like God before,
and now we see that this is a much better life;
henceforth, we will never go back to the old life.
We as people of the world
need this Mighty Change
to be able to progress and live
with God again; without temptation.

# THE WORLD

## L. TALMAGE GORRINGE

The world is a magnificent place: It provides food, shelter,
and a safe haven from harm and danger.
when you feast upon The Word of God,
you begin to understand why this life is important to all mankind;
to be united with the things of nature for our good;
to build refuges and safe Havens,
that no one will be left unprotected from nature's wrath,
or from Satan, the Devil.
We, united, will build refuges and safe havens for those who are unable,
to give them protection and homes to dwell in for time and all eternity.

## WILD EYES

L. TALMAGE GORRINGE

The people who have wild eyes are fearless,
full of character, and love to take risks.
Wild Eyes like to have fun,
even to the extent of getting hurt in the process;
they love the feel of Adrenalin rushing through their system.
When people receive the Wild Eyes' sensation,
they are always on the go and like to take risks.
Sometimes when people receive Wild Eyes,
they become daredevils,
and sometimes they scare the people around them
so much that their friends will try to talk you out of doing something
dangerous like skydiving or something else.

## FIRE EYES

L. TALMAGE GORRINGE

When you receive a burning sensation in your eyes,
you will feel like you can succeed beyond
your potential and will help people along the way.
Fire Eyes can make you do things faster than you can handle,
and push you beyond your maximum potential, for the good of others;
so be careful, and always be in control.
I love it when I receive Fire Eyes
because I then know that our Father is helping me find
the skills and the experience I need
to succeed beyond my own potential.

## SEARCH TO SEARCH

L. TALMAGE GORRINGE

When ye search with a determination,
to find the truth,
ye must search with faith wanting
to receive by faith the answers to
your questions or curiosities,
whether it be good or whether it be evil.
Search to Search, to find yourself
and to bring peace and happiness
to your heart and soul.
When ye search, search with a pure intent
wanting to learn of the mysteries of Heaven
and Earth; the glorious blessings
of all mankind.

## TEACH TO TEACH

L. TALMAGE GORRINGE

As ye teach, teach with the spirit
a nd everything will go
according to God's plan.
Teach to teach, to improve yourself
and those around you,
to bring exaltation and eternal life unto other's s ouls.
When you teach, teach with power and conviction,
that you may know with a surety that what you teach is correct and true,
to help you succeed in life and in the life to come.
Teach to teach, with a passion that no one can copy or deny.

# THE TASTE OF DEATH

### L. Talmage Gorringe

The taste of death is usually painful and you suffer much;

but some have a quick and painless death,

a death that calls up your soul to teach

and administer the gospel of Jesus Christ

in the Spirit World,

to give others one more chance

to accept the gospel of Jesus Christ

and be saved

in the kingdom of God.

When ye receive the painful agony of death,

ye will be happy,

hence, ye will be

one step closer to receiving immortality,

exaltation, and eternal life;

for without death,

life cannot come,

and ye will not be redeemed from the Fall of Adam.

Hence, ye will dwell in sin forever more.

The taste of death is cruel and unusual punishment,

that bringeth you to ask

"Why me, Why now,

Isn't there

An easier

Way?"

# SERVE TO SERVE

L. TALMAGE GORRINGE

When ye serve your fellow man,

ye are serving God with faith, commitment,

and power, to bring peace and happiness to your soul,

to give unto them a glimpse of eternal life

in the Celestial Kingdom.

Serve to Serve, and ye will not be tempted

or harmed by the adversary or

the cunning deceptions of the world.

As ye serve in righteousness,

ye cannot sin or transgress against God the Father,

hence, ye are perfect for an instant,

but only an instant.

Serve to serve,

and receive all glory to your name.

# THE ADVOCATE

L. Talmage Gorringe
(Jesus Christ)

The Advocate pleads to save lives,

to bring unto them a Celestial life,

a life of knowledge and wisdom,

that will put exaltation and eternal life

back into their sphere for all eternity.

Fathers and Mothers are Advocates to their family and friends,

whom they love and care for deeply,

to help bring them to the highest degree of the Celestial

Kingdom,

where God, the Father and His Son, Jesus Christ, dwell,

where ye will be truly happy.

The Advocate stands in to save a troubled soul,

that all may be forgiven,

to prosper toward

the highest degree of glory

(the Celestial Glory,)

the glory of the sun.

## THE ARMOR OF GOD

L. TALMAGE GORRINGE

The Armor of God
shields you from danger;
it has the power to block out or
completely get rid of evil temptations
by helping us think good and righteous thoughts.
As you learn how to put on the Armor of God,
you come to have a closer relationship with the Father,
one that cannot be destroyed.
The Armor of God protects you from physical,
emotional, spiritual, and mental temptations.
When you wear the Armor of God,
it lets people know that ye have
a personal relationship with the Father,
and He will not let anything
harm you.


## THE FIRE WITHIN

L. TALMAGE GORRINGE

The fire within helps complete the Celestial body,
whereby ye understand in every aspect how the body functions,
for without the light or a body there is no way for you to enter into the Celestial Kingdom,
for it will be out of your reach;
when you understand how our Father came to the knowledge of the Celestial Kingdom, which
lead him to become a God, you can strive to do likewise, and never be alone
as you keep the fire burning strong and bright,
you will be protected and kept alive for eternity.

## LOOK TO THE HEART

L. TALMAGE GORRINGE

Look to the heart and ye will find answers;
answers to prayers, to life's questions and curiosities,
and to the mysteries of Heaven and Earth,
and all other blessings from the Holy Ghost,
Jesus Christ, and The Father.
If ye look to the heart, ye will find your true self,
the self which will take you to the Celestial Kingdom,
(The Highest of all Kingdoms);
to dwell with God, the Father and his Son,
Jesus Christ, for eternity,
to live in happiness forever and ever.
Look to the heart
and ye will be happy
for eternity.

## PERSON TO PERSON

L. TALMAGE GORRINGE

When you share your experiences with others,
you understand one another and become personal, best friends.
As a person learns from their own good and bad experiences,
he will be able to help his friends
in time of need or just be there
to listen to and hearken to his troubles and problems of life.
When a person finds others who will be friends,
they will return and befriend you.

# THE ARMY OF GOD

L. TALMAGE GORRINGE

The Army of God bringeth forth His righteous ways,

by destroying the evil in the world now and forever.

As God prepares His army,

he prepares the world,

that they may hearken

and feel a change of heart and become like God,

pure and peaceful like no mortal person is,

to bring perfection and eternal life to their souls.

The Army of God wrought the world from evil,

that God may bring forth the Celestial Kingdom,

the highest and the most glorious Kingdom known to man,

to enhance the unity and love that is shared with all the world.

This army is righteous and spiritual,

to fight for God in behalf of the

righteous dominions that one

father's faithful followers.

# ZION'S LIGHT

L. Talmage Gorringe

Zion's Light is bursting forth,

bringing peace to the righteous,

sharing love from person to person

'til everyone has felt

the Light of Zion forever and ever,

without end.

As the Light of Zion shines,

it will protect you from harm,

evil, and the temptations of the world.

Zion's Light builds you up,

to share love, peace, and joy to all,

that the world may comprehend

and feel of the Light and Life of Zion,

that you may seek and discover

the Light of Zion and

the power it has over the earth.

Let Zion's Light shine,

and nothing will harm you.

# THE GLORY OF GOD

L. TALMAGE GORRINGE

The Glory of God feasts upon

"The Spirit of Truth and Righteousness,"

and His righteous dealings.

When I partake of the Glory of God,

be assured that His Glory will protect my family and me,

from danger, and pain from the Evil One, who is Satan.

The Glory of God is true, in all works of righteousness

and purity, to bring perfection and exaltation to the soul.

As we become more like God the Father,

we will receive His Spirit and Glory,

that nothing will keep us

from the highest degree of all,

(the Celestial Glory),

the Glory of God.

# THE BIRTH OF CHRIST

L. TALMAGE GORRINGE

The birth of Christ shows blood, water,
and sacrifice for all the world to watch and discover,
that they may be saved at the last days,
through the blood and sacrifice of
the Lamb of God.
When the birth of Christ came about,
the world wondered what marvelous and righteous
thing had happened for their sakes.
The birth of Christ comes through
and by blood,
sacrifice,
and living the commandments
and laws of our living God,
the Father.

# STRIFE

L. TALMAGE GORRINGE

Strife bringeth sorrow and sin,
to all who dwell on it; it will bring condemnation to the soul.
If ye don't resolve the strife,
ye will condemn your soul to Outer Darkness,
where Satan dwells.
Strife bringeth problems, problems bringeth error,
error bringeth condemnation with pain and suffering without end.
As ye realize strife exists in your life,
don't despair, God is there waiting to help you resolve this strife,
that ye may become happy without error.

# STRIPPED FROM THE TRUTH

### L. TALMAGE GORRINGE

When ye are stripped from the truth,
ye are forced to let go and allow your family and friends to bring happiness and love to your soul;
the pain and suffering only lasts for a short time, once it starts.
Without being stripped from the truth
ye cannot see the beauty of the mysteries of God,
Heaven, and Earth.
For when ye are stripped, ye will see all the glorious and prosperous blessings in your life, which
our Father loves to bless you with.
Now, after being stripped from the truth,
ye must turn your heart and soul to God the Father,
that He may lead you to a prosperous and successful life.
A life like no other, it is yours and God's, and no other.
Then, and only then, you will be lifted up,
to be glorified and exalted unto
the Most High God
of your very soul, (The Celestial Kingdom.)

# BROTHER TO BROTHER

### L. TALMAGE GORRINGE

When one brother experiences what another teaches, he ought not waste any time to share
his experiences with those whom he loves and cares deeply about.
As one brother acquires life experiences, ye should go and thank his Father and Brother
for teaching him how to receive personal experiences that will lead him back to our
Father's presence, to dwell with him for eternity.
When one brother builds up the other, they both prosper and receive a portion of God's
glory to bring them to prosperity and a pure and righteous understanding with one another.

# REWARD

L. TALMAGE GORRINGE

The reward of your life is the Celestial Kingdom,
the highest of all kingdoms,
one where ye can be happy forever with your family and friends.
When people achieve some great task,
they feel a sense of accomplishment and a job well done,
that, in the worldly sense, is their reward.
The reward that you accomplish,
makes you feel as if you can
do anything anywhere no matter what the situation is,
and that makes you feel great.
When people receive a reward,
they feel like sharing the achievement
with all they see and come in contact with,
to bring happiness
to themselves and others for eternity.

# COWARDS

L. TALMAGE GORRINGE

What makes a coward a coward?
To be cowardly is to not even try;
to live a lonesome quiet life,
to not let anyone help you in your time of need.
Cowardlyness is to not back down from a challenge,
even though your opponent may hurt you badly or worse, kill you.
To use not your brain to get out of situations;
to resolve crucial yet dangerous situations
by talking about the conflict and resolving
in a calm and highly confident manner.

# WALK

L. Talmage Gorringe

Walk in steadfastness with God,

feast upon the Will of the Father.

When ye walk with the Father,

ye are immortal and

exalted like unto our Father,

with whom ye will dwell for eternity.

Walk is to walk and not faint,

to run and not be weary,

to feast and not be

tempted by the devil,

who is Satan.

As ye walk, don't walk to walk,

but walk in our Father's footsteps

walk to look forward and to look back.

When ye walk, walk uprightly and with faith,

and no unclean thing will enter by way of sin.

Walk with faith, and you'll always be close to our Father.

# PRESS FORWARD

L. TALMAGE GORRINGE

Press forward with faith, determination,

and a plan in your heart.

As we look forward

with steadfastness of heart,

we press forward with that

which bringeth forth our eternal plan

and salvation to our lives.

Pressing forward,

enduring to the end of our lives,

we must be faithful

unto our Heavenly Father

and our forefathers,

that we may return in good

faith with joy in our hearts,

that we may dwell in

the Kingdom of God

with our Father

for eternity.

# THE DIVINE POWER

### L. TALMAGE GORRINGE

The Divine Power

can raise a man from the dead,

or save a child from a burning building,

that he may have no burns on his body.

As I use the Divine Power,

I grow closer

to our Father,

and become as he is

(a God,) knowing all things,

good and evil,

and having control over what I do;

I cannot be tempted by Satan, the Devil.

The Divine Power keeps me alive,

that I may achieve mine divine destiny,

that I may receive the opportunity

to live with

our Father in Heaven again,

for eternity.

# THE DIVINE DESTINY

## L. Talmage Gorringe

The Divine Destiny comes from within;
it can lead us back to our Father's presence,
to bring exaltation and eternal life to the soul,
that we may dwell with our Father
in the Celestial Kingdom
for eternity.
When we find our Divine Destiny,
we will have learned exactly
how to return to our
Father's presence
in glory,
and joy, forever and ever without end.
The Divine Destiny will bring peace, joy,
and happiness to the soul,
that we may dwell in perfection with God our Father.
What does it take to find your Divine Destiny?
You must search your soul
and bring inspiration and faith back into your life;
then you may receive your Divine Destiny;
The destiny which leads you
to our
Father's presence,
to dwell with him
for eternity.

Join My Heavenly Throng

## GOD'S WILL FOR TAL GORRINGE

As Dusty and I struggle back up the sleigh riding hill, we watch Tal go down. Tal is a gutsy five year old. He wanted to tackle that gigantic hill all by himself. The glad-a-boggen is heading straight down the hill. What's going on? Tal's Sled is turning. It's going under the hand rail. I hope Tal doesn't hit the hand rail. Crash!

"That's my son. My son is hurt! Can you take my baby Grandma?"

Half skating, half sliding, and clinging to the handrail, I finally got to my son. My Tal.

I picked his limp body up and carefully carried him down the hill. It's probably a mild concussion. Tommy had three of those. Tommy's O.K.

My hands are red. Blood. Oh no. I'd better put Tal down. What if something is broken?

"Call an ambulance! Someone call an ambulance!"

He's bleeding from his nose and mouth. My Tal. My Tal. Margene, clean an air passage. His jaw is locked shut. You've got to pry his mouth open. Stick your thumb in his mouth. He is still breathing.

There's a big circle of people around. People who were sleigh riding just minutes ago, are now in a prayer circle around us. A lady is saying a prayer. Where's a priesthood holder?

Please, is there a priesthood holder?

A woman, who says she is a nurse, is putting a blanket over Tal. She is trying to put keys between his teeth so my fingers won't be bitten off. At least I'm doing something. A man is coming this way.

"Will you administer to my son?"

What is the man saying?

"Bless this young boy that he will live until the doctors can help him."

That's not enough. Bless him again.

O.K. Heavenly Father, bless Tal to be O.K.

Finally, the paramedics are here. They stabilize his head. Paramedics can't transfer? A Gold Cross ambulance is necessary to take Tal to the hospital? I hear it coming. Heavenly Father, help Tal. Bless him to live. Bless him to be O.K.

What started out to be a fun family sleigh ride outing at Sugarhouse Park has turned out to be . . .

Grandma is taking the other four kids.

"Linda, tell Gary we'll be at Holy Cross Hospital."

I don't want to be in front of the ambulance. I want to be with Tal. Can't I get in the back with Tal? Heavenly Father, bless Tal to live. Heavenly Father, bless Tal to be O.K.

Oh no! Problems. We can't go to Holy Cross Hospital. The Cat Scan isn't working. Heavenly Father are you helping?

Can Tal last the extra distance to Primary Children's Hospital?

Heavenly Father, are you there?

The sirens are blasting. The cars are being considerate and moving out of the way. It still seems like forever. We're crawling. I don't dare look at my son. Maybe they won't tell me if he's dead. How much blood can a little guy lose? Heavenly Father, help us, hurry!

The doors of the hospital clank open. Tal is whisked into an emergency room. I see only a glimpse of him.

"Is he still alive?"

They lead me into a small waiting room. Gary, doesn't know we're here.

"Can someone let Gary know where we are?"

A doctor says they will call Holy Cross Hospital. They will let Gary know Tal is at Primary Children's Hospital.

A doctor asks, what's Tal's blood type: "I don't know."

They'll use universal donor blood. Why don't I know that? It could save his life.

Will Gary blame me? What will I do if Gary blames me? Can I face him?

Two policemen are entering the room. How can I talk to them. I'm barely holding myself together.

O.K. Margene, stop your crying long enough to answer the policemen's questions.

What's his name?

What's your name?

What's your husband's name?

Where do you live?

Where did it happen?

What time? I don't know. What time is it anyway?

"About 4:00, I guess. I don't know. A half hour ago."

Where's Gary? Shouldn't he be here by now? Is he going to blame me?

I need to find someone to administer to Tal. Maybe that man can help me. He looks like a security guard. Good. He's going to find some oil. Tal doesn't look like Tal with tubes coming out of him, and his head shaven. The man says if Gary doesn't want to give the blessing because of the way Tal looks, he will find someone else.

Where's Gary?

Will he blame me? I need to call someone in the ward. The Bishop is out of town over Christmas holidays. I'll call Dennis Lumbardi. I know his number. Where's a phone?

"Hello Dennis."

Margene, stop crying. He can't understand you.

"Tal's been hurt real bad; the doctors are trying to stabilize him. We're at Primary Children's Hospital. Oh Dennis . . ."

I hang up. It may be rude but I can't talk anymore. Here's Gary.

"Do you blame me?"

Tears stream down my face. His arms encircle me.

"Of course not"

Once I get control, I will tell Gary the details. I immediately direct him to the security guard who has the oil. Again, the security guard cautions Gary, it might be best to have someone else administer to Tal because of all the tubes.

Gary hasn't seen Tal yet, but chooses to administer the blessing himself. Gary returns. The realization of the seriousness staggers him.

The doctors come out. A wall of white approaches us. Their faces display great concern. I don't know if I want to hear what they're going to say.

"Tal has lost a lot of blood. He is in a life threatening situation. There is a paralysis on the right side. We're trying to stabilize him enough to take him to the CAT Scan, then to surgery."

Dr. Walker warns us that Tal won't live unless they operate, and he might not live through the operation. Tal's skull is cracked from his nose all the way back to the base of his skull. The surgery could take six or seven hours.

Brother Lumbardi, from the bishopric and brother Elsby come to comfort us. I so much appreciate them being here.

Still in his hospital scrub suit, Dr. Walker is coming to talk to us. It's only 7:00 P.M. It only took two hours. The operation is over. They have removed the whole left side of his skull, which is in four or five big pieces and could be replaced later. The fragmented skull cut into the motor area, the speech area, and a little into the vision area.

The critical concern now is the swelling of his brain. Tal's pulse rate has been irregular all night. When it reaches 200, an alarm goes off. A machine shows Tal's brain waves are going wild. I don't know what it means except it doesn't worry me. I know what it means to have a flat brain line. Activity, no matter how erratic indicates Tal's brain is still alive.

Grandma and Grandpa are here with us now, as well as Gary's Mom, his brother, Randy, and niece, Linda. They insist on staying. We sack out on couches, chairs, and the floor. The hospital provides blankets. Between worrying, squeaky chairs, and going to check on Tal, nobody sleeps.

Gary and I finally sent everyone home about 2:00 A.M.

Dr. Walker is sleeping in a little room next to ICU, so he can be there if Tal needs help.

During the night I visit Tal several times. This time the nurse tells me she doesn't know how long Tal can last like this. She tells me to talk to Tal; he can probably hear me. I talk to him and cry. I tell him how much I love him, and that I will fight for him as long as he wants me to keep fighting.

I went back to Gary after this visit with tears streaming.

"Gary, I feel Tal is listening to me from Heaven. I picture him holding Heavenly Father's hand as I tell him how much I love him."

I visit Tal maybe once more that eternal night. It is hard to see my son with his head shaved, swollen like a balloon, and so disfigured. Tubes here, Ivy's there. No clothes on his little body.

Not moving. Tal doesn't look like that! Maybe it is a comfort to me to envision him holding Heavenly Father's hand, well, whole, and happy.

Tal made it through the night. That's a good sign. He's still in a life threatening condition.

Another CAT Scan is done this morning. The scan reveals blood clots in the center of the brain, and one that has saturated the frontal lobe and destroyed it. Another operation. How much can Tal handle? The probability of Tal not making it through the operation is still great. The doctors won't touch the clot in the center of the brain because more damage could occur from cutting than the blood clot itself. The frontal lobe needs to be removed. The thoughts of having part of Tal's brain removed crushes Gary and me. Was Tal going to end up a vegetable after all this?

The third clot won't require cutting into the brain and can be easily removed.

Prayers fill my heart and mind again. I know Heavenly Father is here. His arms seem to sooth me like a cradle song. I know he guides the doctors' hands. As long as Heavenly Father is with Tal, I can accept whatever happens. What is God's Will for Tal? He helped Tal stay alive 'til the doctors could attend to him as promised in the blessing. (We realize now it was a blessing for the paramedics to detour to Primary Children's Hospital. Dr. Walker is the best pediatric neurosurgeon in the West. Was Dr. Walker at Primary Children's hospital by chance?)

The doctors return and Gary and I are overwhelmed by another miracle. The clot that was discovered on the CAT Scan to have saturated the frontal lobe, turns out to be only a surface clot.

It is easily removed with no more damage to the brain. Thank you Heavenly Father. Thank you!

What is God's Will for my son? He wants Tal to live! Tal is a determined little guy. Whatever God's Will is, Tal can handle it. Tal will live and love and be happy no matter what the circumstances are, and I can too.